M000019384

the Healthy Witch

Designed by Brenda McCallum

Type set in Fenice/Minion

ISBN: 978-0-7643-5790-9
Printed in China

Published by Red Feather Mind, Body, Spirit
An imprint of Schiffer Publishing, Ltd.
4880 Lower Valley Road | Atglen, PA 19310
Phone: (610) 593-1777; Fax: (610) 593-2002
E-mail: Info@schifferbooks.com
Web: www.redfeathermbs.com

For our complete selection of fine books on this and related subjects, please visit our website at www.schifferbooks.com. You may also write for a free catalog.

Schiffer Publishing's titles are available at special discounts for bulk purchases for sales promotions or premiums. Special editions, including personalized covers, corporate imprints, and excerpts, can be created in large quantities for special needs. For more information, contact the publisher.

We are always looking for people to write books on new and related subjects.
If you have an idea for a book, please contact us at proposals@schifferbooks.com.

the *Healthy Witch*

A Workbook for Optimal Health

TJ Perkins

REDFeather™

MIND | BODY | SPIRIT

4880 Lower Valley Road, Atglen, PA 19310

AUTHOR NOTE

TJ Perkins is not a licensed physician, nor is she a nutrition expert. She has been practicing Wicca for thirteen years and has achieved the status of second degree and Journeywoman.

All findings are from trial and error, years of being in pain, and finding the answers in a holistic way. She has sought out many professionals and went through years of experimenting, trying new techniques, and trusting in the Goddess. Finally, with pain diminishing and digestive symptoms improving, the truth has been revealed and TJ now shares all that she's learned with you.

Still, don't take everything for granted in this field guide—do your own research, ask questions, and experiment.

CONTENTS

Chapter 1

MIND, BODY, HEALTH—
THE PATH

OMG, is this another diet book?

No. I would not do that to you.

Think of this book as a guide to being the best Witch you can possibly be. The Goddess wants us to be our best—as within, so without. But how can you be your very best if your body is miserable? How can you meditate if your legs fall asleep, your knees hurt, or you have low back and neck pain? How can you mentally connect if you're more focused on all of your bodily aches and pains rather than visualization and ritual? If you have chronic neck pain, stomach upset, and other physical problems that take away the zest for life, how can you ignore them and rejoin all the wonderful feelings of being a part of the Goddess and this amazing Earth?

Answer—you can't. And if you can, then you've achieved a high level of mental focus that most people just can't reach.

For the rest of us, I have answers. And for the answers I don't have, you will be guided to figure them out on your own.

Throughout most of my adult life I have been in pain—most through no fault of my own, and the rest of it was inflicted upon me. In my quest over the past thirty years to find relief of my misery I've come upon many techniques and suggestions, doctor visits, do this, try that . . . most were only short-term help. Then I discovered others that were more long term, but even those fizzled out without additional support. With additional support came additional expense. Most of us cannot afford all the doctor visits.

Most of us have tried chiropractic and acupuncture. Yes, these techniques can help, but only to a certain point. You'll plateau and find yourself going every week for the same treatment with no further pain relief or results. Weeks turn into months, which turn into years, until you finally realize you're just spinning your wheels.

I encourage you to continue to exercise; do Tai Chi and yoga, run on that treadmill, push through the pain, and, especially, go to massage therapy. Keep in mind that it won't completely fix the problem, but those physical activities are a partner to healing. Just like your BEN-GAY®, ChryoDerm®, and other creams, gels, and pills.

As a Witch I fully believe in the Goddess and that everything happens for a reason. At first I couldn't fathom why I was going though the pain for so many years. And then I found an all-new chiropractic treatment the Activator Method.

St. John's Wort

Unlike the typical twisting/cracking of usual chiropractic treatments, the Activator is a spring-loaded metal device that is gentle and nonevasive, used to pinpoint a single vertebra and a very small area of your back, neck, etc. at a time, not a whole section of the back. Because of the instrument's speed, the muscles that are treated are less likely to tense up. This means a patient could be more receptive to treatment.

This method is the only thing that has been able to give me relief of my pain. But it didn't last long, and like always, I plateau. There must be something else I could do.

A few years later I started to feel pain in every muscle all over my body. It started in one area, then spread to another, then another, and suddenly it spread all over like an infection. This was an all-new type of pain, and through holistic Nutrition Response Testing and supplements, with my Activator chiropractor, we discovered that it was actually things I had been eating that were the cause of my muscle inflammation.

I began to understand how amazing it was that even the simplest things we eat could harm us. What we take in affects our organs, and all organs are connected and affect each other. I then started to realize that every organ in our body relates to the elements, which relates to the pentagram, which relates to practice as a Witch.

A few years ago a good friend of mine introduced me to the Dragon's Way, an ancient technique of exercise and flushing out the body of toxins in a six-week regimen. Using specific exercise movements, and stopping the consumption of most everything you ingest all at one time, this technique requires the utmost discipline. Most people will not stick with this, but it clearly showed me how Chinese medicine, and the Dragon's Way, related to Pagan beliefs as well.

We are connected to all the elements, and each organ has a very specific place in the pentagram. They interact and interrelate to every part of the body and affect your health. What happens to one part of the pentagram could tear down the other parts. I want to show you how to find a healthy balance, using all that I have learned, and relating it to the Craft. Now let's begin:

YOU

There is an old Zen adage: Ken-Zen Ichi Nyo ("Body and Mind Together"). You cannot separate the mental and magikal processes from the physical ones. Magikal energy will flow best if your body is in good shape. Everything in your environment—mental, physical, emotional, and spiritual—affects how you raise energy and how this energy affects you and your magikal output.

AS WITHIN + SO WITHOUT = THE BEST WITCH YOU CAN BE

Take a moment to list your physical issues from head to toe. Use the section below. Start with your head. Here you will list things such as migraines, constant eye infections, dry eye, hair falling out, TMJ, etc. As we move down the body, list only problems with skin, organs, brittle nails, etc. Do not worry about weight! We all have weight issues, and as we work through this handbook and fix US, the weight will fix itself.

Head: ....

....

....

Neck: ....

....

....

Shoulders/Arms/Hands: ....

....

....

....

....

Chest: ....

....

....

Torso: ....

....

....

Hips/Upper Legs: ....

....

....

Legs/Feet: ....

....

....

The 13 Goals of a Witch

BY SCOTT CUNNINGHAM

1. Know thyself.

2. Know thy Craft.

3. Learn; knowledge is power.

4. Apply knowledge with wisdom.

5. Achieve balance in your life and everything around you.

6. Keep your words in good order; negativity breeds negativity.

7. Keep your thoughts in good order.

8. Celebrate life and all the stages of it.

9. Attune with the cycle of the Earth and Moon.

10. Breathe and eat correctly.

11. Exercise the body as well as the spirit.

12. Meditate everyday.

13. Honor the Goddess and God.

Now, why did I list this? Well, look at numbers 5, 10, 11, and 12. This field guide will help you achieve many of these goals. As for the rest— that's up to you.

As women we are made up of all the elements. These elements are what make our world alive. Remove just one element and life cannot exist. The Goddess is the essential Being, and Her energy is connected to each element. We, in turn, are a part of Her. Our soul purpose in this Plane is to become the best Witch possible, building our energy (within/ without) and rising to a higher vibration level so when our body dies, our energies will return to Her. So, we must make Her stronger with each of our lifetimes. Remember, She is the world and all the elements and all the energies from past, present, and future.

In order for us to pass unto Her the best energy possible, WE need to be the best we can be NOW. And we can't do that unless we're happy with ourselves and are healthy enough to meditate, pray, conduct ritu- als, be physically active, and just plain enjoy life.

The Witch of today leans toward herbs for healing, incense for calming, and trying to, in general, eat healthfully. We all crave for something that provides a sense of goodness. Don't let the doctors keep telling you that you need a pill for this pain, or that migraine, or you need mental health care. Depending on the diagnosis, you may really need medicine, but that's not always the case.

What I've discovered is that all you need is what you already have deep inside. You just need to use it a different way. Herbs and using our witchy-ness are parts of our primal urge to reconnect with our wild natures and heal ourselves. Our goal is to find peace and comfort. You can do that without spending a lot of money and wasting time at doctor visits or taking medicine you don't really need. Reach deep within yourself and ferret out the elements and their inner connection to all that you are.

Every woman is born a witch. It's up to you to Awaken and heal.

Chapter 2

THE ELEMENTS AS THEY PERTAIN TO YOU

Here is the pentagram. As we all know, it represents the elements. But have you ever thought about how the elements relate to your body and organs and how all that connects to your digestion problems and physical ailments? Let me show you.

SPIRIT

The top of the pentagram is Spirit. This is where the **liver and gallbladder** preside.

The gallbladder is the liver's partner organ and is integral to the harmonious function of the body.

The liver has control of the heart and a little less control over the kidney. If the liver is taxed to the point where it cannot filter out the toxins going in, then that will cause liver failure. Once liver failure begins, trouble for the heart, kidney, and thyroid shortly follow. Fix the liver and you'll fix the heart, kidney, and thyroid.

How do I know if I have the beginnings of liver failure?

Over all, body aches and pain accompanied by excessive amounts of trigger points in your muscles, legs, and glutes. If these muscles are hot to the touch, or hurt when barely touched, then they are inflamed. Reason: If your liver is so overworked and cannot flush out toxins, then those toxins back up into your body. They get into your cells, which go into your bloodstream, which goes to your muscles, and then the muscles will cramp/spasm, thus causing you overall body aches and pain. EVERYTHING will hurt (low back, T-bands, knees, neck, arms, etc.).

Lavender

How do I know if my liver is not happy?

✳ All-over muscle pain, muscle inflammation, muscle cramping

✳ Burning or irritation of the eyes

✳ Tendon problems

✳ Migraines (left side of head)

✳ Indigestion and bloating

✳ Stress

✳ Yeast infections

✳ Excess weight

✳ Cold hands and feet

✳ Menstrual problems / PMS / menopause

What causes liver failure?

✳ Taking medicine for long periods of time. This can be prescriptions or even Tylenol'.

✳ Food allergies. Sometimes you won't even know it! Eggs and shellfish are notorious culprits. Try eliminating these from your diet for six weeks and see how you feel. If that doesn't work, try eliminating dairy, sugar, or caffeine (or a combination of these).

✳ Toxins—from the foods you eat

✳ Certain herbal supplements—kava, ephedra, skullcap, and pennyroyal, have been linked to acute liver failure.

✳ Hepatitis and other viruses

Dandelion

Magikal Associations

* **Eye:** This is the sense organ related to the liver.

* **Tendons:** They should be kept flexible. Make sure to stretch every day!

* **Spring:** Stay calm during spring, and don't get caught up in these new energies.

* **Wind** is the environmental factor.

* **Green** is the color.

* **Sour** is the taste. Do you crave sour-tasting things?

* **East** is the direction (though spirit is all around us, we're talking about the liver direction).

* **Anger** is the emotion. If you are easy to anger, feel irritable, or have problems "going with the flow," you are experiencing a liver function problem.

* **Liver and gallbladder** energy dominates between the hours of 11:00 p.m. and 3:00 a.m. Do you find yourself getting up to go to the bathroom, waking up / tossing and turning, or simply just can't fall asleep during that time period?

* Tarot card: **Justice.**

* Crystal: **Phantom**—clear, red, or yellow. Very powerful tool for the New Age. In healing work it's used to disperse congested energies. Yellow Apatite: treats the liver, pancreas, gallbladder, and spleen.

Just as your liver's job is to keep the flow of energy and blood running smoothly, it must keep your emotions flowing evenly as well. Our bodies were created so our organs work in harmony, our life energy flows, and we are in balance. If your liver is healthy then your gallbladder will be healthy.

We all know stress has a direct influence on your health and weight. Too much for an excessive period of time and our bodies become sluggish, which directly affects your weight.

How Can I Fix My Liver/Gallbladder Issues?

Are you ready for this? I know you can do it.
Here are some suggestions:

* Lay off soda and snacks (chips of any kind, fast foods, candy, etc.).

* Discontinue anything that has fructose, high fructose, or corn syrup. Yes, it's in so much of the stuff we eat, and it's horrible for your body. You see, these things are man-made sugars, and when you ingest them, your body doesn't know what to do with them—so they're stored in your fat cells. Ewww! The more you ingest, the more is stored until you begin to balloon up. Many of us are allergic to fructose and don't even know it. If your intestines cramp, or your "belly" gets hard, or you feel suddenly bloated or very gassy, chances are that you're allergic.

* Stay active; go for a brisk walk (not a casual stroll), lift weights, do yoga, stretch. Join a gym, or set up a little workout area in your home—anything to release anger and aggressions in a healthy way and keep your blood flowing.

* Meditate.

* Go for massage therapy.

* Drink dandelion tea and eat arugula. These bitters naturally detox the liver.

* Cut back on alcohol. Now I'm not saying you can't have a glass of wine from time to time, but don't polish off a bottle every night or slug down a six-pack every week.

🔑 Remember: Everything in moderation; find your balance in ALL THINGS.

Spirit/Spring
Liver/Gallbladder
Ostara/Beltane/Spring Equinox

Air

Water

Earth

Fire

No one knows your body like you. Take a moment now to list some troubled traits of the liver and gallbladder that you've noticed within yourself:

....

....

....

....

....

....

....

....

....

....

PLAN OF ACTION

Okay, so what should I start doing to fix my liver/gallbladder issues? Make a list of things that you can AND WILL do. Suggestion: Do a liver cleanse. You can drink dandelion tea and incorporate arugula into your salads or on your sandwich. A full liver cleanse will take about six weeks.

....

....

....

....

....

....

....

....

....

EARTH

The bottom left corner of the pentagram is Earth. This is where the **stomach and spleen** preside. The spleen is actually connected to the lungs and heart. If the spleen is in good health, then the heart will not have any problems.

The Earth energy of the spleen and stomach helps control the kidney like a dam controls water. If they are weak, then your kidney will be weak, and the end result will be that your body will retain too much water/fluid.

The stomach is the main organ related to weight gain. Stomach energy is the food you eat (take in). Through eating and drinking, you constantly create energy coming in and energy going out. If your digestive system is not functioning properly, you will not be able to get enough nutrition, or make sufficient energy, to meet your body's daily energy needs. You want a balance.

No matter how many healthy foods you eat, if your spleen or stomach doesn't function properly, your body can't take the food and transform it into the energy it needs.

Your immune system is located in the lining of the stomach. One of the biggest causes of a weakened immune system has to do with the over-abundant amounts of sugar that are in everything we eat. Sugar is what impairs your immune system, resulting in it being easier for unwanted viruses and bacteria to fester longer than they should.

Chives

How do I know if my spleen or stomach isn't happy?

* Bloating, upset, cramping
* Poor sleep
* Bruising easily
* Migraines (center of forehead)
* High cholesterol levels
* Allergies (it's not the food you eat but your stomach that has the problem)
* Lack of energy
* Lack of appetite
* Your left eye waters—your stomach and left eye are connected. If you ingest anything that you're allergic to, only your left eye will water. If you use a lotion or makeup that your body has an issue with, your left eye will water. It takes ten seconds for anything you put on your body to enter the blood stream and quickly go to your organs. It takes three days for anything that you've taken into your body to get filtered out (except a steak dinner).

What causes stomach or spleen failure?

* **Enlarged Spleen.** An enlarged spleen can be caused by infections, cirrhosis, and other liver diseases; blood diseases characterized by abnormal blood cells; problems with the lymph system; or other conditions.

❋ **Digestive Disorders.** This is what the stomach has to deal with—in all its forms, such as IBS (irritable-bowel syndrome). What you put into your body is what you're made up of. You know the old saying "You are what you eat"? It's so true!

Here is a list of foods you can eat that will help boost your immune system: grapefruit, oranges, tangerines, lemons, limes, clementines, red bell peppers, broccoli, garlic, ginger, spinach, yogurt, almonds, turmeric, green tea, papaya, kiwi, chicken, turkey, shellfish.

Also use herbs and spices such as thyme, rosemary, basil, cloves, oregano, and ginger; oils such as coconut oil, olive oil, sesame oil, and flax oil; and beverages such as chicory root coffee, cinnamon tea, peppermint tea, ginger tea, and licorice.

MAGIKAL ASSOCIATIONS

❋ **Mouth**: the sense organ related to the spleen and stomach
❋ **Muscles**: A muscle problem also signifies a stomach problem.
❋ **Worry/overthinking**: too much
❋ **Late summer**: This is the spleen's season.
❋ The environmental factor is **Dampness.**
❋ **Yellow**: This is the associated color.
❋ **Sweet**: The associated taste. Do you crave sweets?
❋ **Middle/Center**: the direction. (Though Earth sits in the north, we're talking about the spleen direction.)

Fern

❊ Spleen and stomach energies dominate between the hours of **7:00 a.m. and 11:00 a.m.** Do you have cramps after breakfast, or after drinking coffee/tea? Do you skip breakfast because you're not hungry?

❊ Tarot card: **Chariot** for the stomach

❊ Crystal: **Pyrite**—aids digestion, improves circulation. Strengthens and oxygenates blood. Enhances brain functions. Influences a more positive outlook on life. Enhances emotional body, strengthens will. **Rhodochrosite**—aids spleen, kidneys, heart, pituitary gland, and circulation of blood.

HOW CAN I FIX MY LIVER/GALLBLADDER ISSUES?

I'm glad you asked, but this is no easy task. You will have to be disciplined in your endeavors. Here are some suggestions:

❊ Eat foods that are warm. Why? Because it takes less energy to digest cooked food, rather than raw.

❊ Do not drink cold liquids, especially if you're overheated. Room temperature is best.

❊ Eat more fruit.

❊ Don't eat late at night. Make a plan to stop eating by 7:00 p.m.

❊ Eat slowly, take your time, and when you start to feel even a little bit full—STOP. It takes your body a good ten minutes for food to reach the stomach. Once it does, put down your utensils and chat, wait, and feel your stomach expand with what you gave it. Now, how do you feel? If you are comfortable, take a few more bites. If not, ask for a take-home box.

❋ Drink ginger tea. You don't have to get a specialty tea. Just hot water and fresh ginger slices. Add lemon if you like or a cinnamon stick.

🔑 Remember, everything in moderation.

Spirit/Spring
Liver/Gallbladder
Ostara/Beltane/Spring Equinox

Air

Water

Earth/Late Summer
Spleen/Stomach
Litha

Fire

No one knows your body like you. Take a moment now to list below some troubled traits of the spleen and stomach that you've noticed within yourself:

....

....

....

....

....

....

....

....

....

....

....

PLAN OF ACTION

What should I start doing to fix my spleen/stomach issues? Make a list of things that you can AND WILL do. Suggestion—eat more cooked food. Your body uses up more energy to digest raw food (such as salads) than cooked. You need to keep that energy internal to heal.

....

....

....

....

....

....

....

....

....

WATER

The right side of the pentagram houses water. This is where the **kidney and urinary bladder** preside.

The urinary bladder is the kidney's partner organ and has a close energetic relationship to it.

The kidney is the major organ for your energy and supports the whole body. It's important to learn to save energy and maintain a healthy kidney through optimum digestive function to increase the quality of longevity of your life. The kidney is your storage area of the "food energy" you received from the stomach and spleen, which they in turn got from food and drink.

How do I know if I have the beginnings of kidney failure?

* Increased blood pressure
* Excessive fatigue
* Sleeping troubles
* Feet or ankle swelling (which later progresses upward)
* Forgetfulness and trouble concentrating
* Nausea or vomiting
* Decreased appetite and unintentional weight loss
* Muscle twitching or cramps

Aloe

How do I know if my kidney and bladder are not happy?

- ❋ Loss of hair
- ❋ Forgetfulness
- ❋ Urinating frequently
- ❋ Thyroid problems
- ❋ High blood pressure
- ❋ Ringing in ears

- Always thirsty
- Osteoporosis
- Knee, heel, or neck pain, and chronic lower back pain

What am I doing to cause these issues?

- Too much alcohol and caffeine will affect the kidney and bladder.
- Smoking
- Not exercising and/or maintaining a healthy weight

Magikal Associations

- **Ears**: The sense organs; should be protected from extreme cold during the winter.
- **Bones**: Osteoporosis is an indication that your kidney energy is low and not functioning properly.
- **Fear**: The emotion associated with the kidney
- **Winter**: The kidney's season; its environmental factor is cold.
- **Deep sighing**: The sound associated with the kidney. Do you find yourself doing this a lot?
- **Dark blue or black** is the color.
- **Salty** is the taste. Ever have a sudden craving for pretzels or chips in the afternoon before dinnertime?
- **North** is the direction (though water sits in the west, we're talking about the kidney direction).

❋ Kidney and bladder energy dominates between the hours of **3:00 p.m. and 7:00 p.m.**

❋ Tarot card: **Justice** (kidney) and **Star** (bladder)

❋ Crystal—**Rose Quartz**—aids kidneys and circulatory system. **Smoky Quartz**—strengthens adrenals, kidneys, pancreas. You can also use **Jade**.

Menopause is a time of great change. You go through emotional and physical trauma, gain weight, tire more easily, and slow down. You can't handle stress as well as you used to, and that will affect your organs. This is a time where we need to reinvent ourselves and fight back.

How can I fix my kidney/bladder issues?

❋ Get adequate rest.

❋ Meditate. Sit quietly, listen to restful music, and get in touch with nature.

❋ Salt will help the kidney, but if you have high blood pressure, I would advise against ingesting any.

❋ Eat walnuts, pine nuts, and black sesame seeds.

❋ Eat black beans; use sesame oil and walnut oil.

❋ Drink lots of water, cranberry juice.

❋ Take probiotics and vitamin C.

❋ Consume apples and apple juice.

❋ Take an Epsom salts bath.

Spirit/Spring
Liver/Gallbladder
Ostara/Beltane/Spring Equinox

Air

Water/Winter
Kidney /Urinary
Bladder
Yule/Imbolc

Earth
Late Summer/
Solstice
Spleen/Stomach
Litha

Fire

No one knows your body like you. Take a moment now to list below some troubled traits of the kidney and bladder that you've noticed within yourself:

....

....

....

....

....

....

....

....

....

....

....

Plan of Action

What should I start doing to fix my kidney/bladder issues? Make a list of things that you can AND WILL do. Suggestion—do a kidney cleanse. Drink more water, but don't overdo it. Everything in moderation.

....

....

....

....

....

....

....

....

....

....

AIR

The far left side of the pentagram is Air. This is where the **lungs and large intestine** preside. These two organs have a very close energetic relationship.

The lungs are responsible for the distribution of all your food energy. You don't want this energy to become sluggish. Your body depends on a functioning lung energy system to get all the nutrition to the rest of the body.

How do I know if my lungs or large intestines aren't happy?

※ Shortness of breath

※ Asthma

※ Skin problems

※ A bloated face

※ A cough that doesn't go away or gets worse

※ Hoarseness or wheezing

※ Chest pain

※ Coughing up blood

※ Pneumonia that doesn't go away or that goes away and comes back

What causes lung or large-intestine failure?

※ Smoking

* Eating too many carbs or processed foods
* Toxins or poisons released into your body in the form of mucous or a head cold
* Cancer
* Asthma
* IBS
* Diseases: Crohn's, diverticulosis and diverticulitis, ulcerative colitis, to name just a few.

Chamomile

Magikal Associations

- ✳ **Nose**: the sense organ

- ✳ **Skin**: Our natural protection. It covers our muscles, tendons, organs, etc. If your lungs or large intestines don't have a good energy flow, then your skin will block that energy and the pores will cease to allow toxins to leave your body. It can cause early wrinkles or skin blemishes.

- ✳ **Grief**: The emotion associated with the lung, and **crying** helps you relieve stress.

- ✳ **Autumn** is the season and the environmental factor is **dryness**.

- ✳ **Metal**: the corresponding element

- ✳ **White** is the color.

- ✳ **Spicy** is the taste.

- ✳ The lungs direction is **west** (though Air sits in the east, we're talking about the lung direction).

- ✳ Lung and large-intestine energies dominate between the hours of **3:00 a.m. and 7:00 a.m.**

- ✳ Tarot card: **Lovers** (lungs) and **Death** (large intestines)

- ✳ Crystal: **Moss Agate**—stimulates the digestive process and relieve gastritis. **Anhydrite**—removes retained or excess fluid and disperses swelling.

How can I fix my lung and large intestine issues:

※ Stop smoking.

※ Stop consuming soda, candy, snacks, and anything with fructose, high fructose, or corn syrup.

※ Eat pears, honey, mushrooms, chili, bamboo shoots, scallions, or chestnuts.

※ Consume more home-cooked foods (not fast foods or restaurant foods).

※ Drink more water, but don't overdo it.

Spirit/Spring
Liver/Gallbladder
Ostara/Beltane/Spring Equinox

Air/Autumn
Lungs/Large Intestine
Mabon/Samhain
Fall Equinox

Water/Winter
Kidney /Urinary
Bladder
Yule/Imbolc

Earth
Late Summer/
Solstice
Spleen/Stomach
Litha

Fire

No one knows your body like you. Take a moment now to list below some troubled traits of the lungs and large intestine that you've noticed within yourself:

....

....

....

....

....

....

....

....

....

....

PLAN OF ACTION

What should I start doing to fix my lung/large-intestine issues? Make a list of things that you can AND WILL do. Suggestion—stop smoking. Eat more fruit and vegetables. Everything in moderation.

....

....

....

....

....

....

....

....

....

FIRE

The bottom right corner of the pentagram houses fire. This is where the **heart and small intestines** preside.

Your heart's job is to coordinate all communications between the organs, maintain the proper function, and enable them to work in harmony. Your heart, as well as your liver, controls the circulation of blood in your body. The important energy assignment of the heart is to also control aspects of your mind and emotions.

Many of the problems we associate with the heart are linked to other organs, especially the liver, kidney, and spleen.

How do I know if my heart or small intestine isn't happy?

* High blood pressure
* High cholesterol
* Blocked arteries
* Lack of energy
* Depression
* Anxiety
* Panic attacks or rapid heartbeats
* Bloating, gas, abdominal cramping
* Constipation

What causes heart or small-intestine failure?

❋ Heartburn: caused by stagnate stomach energy

❋ Eating too much and overthinking will cause stomach problems, which will affect the heart.

❋ Lack of exercise

❋ Consuming soda, too much alcohol or caffeine, and all the other bad foods I've mentioned in this handbook

❋ Cancer and other extreme deceases

❋ Infections

❋ IBS

❋ Ulcers (which I blame on stress)

❋ Menopause will cause the heart to beat rapidly. Also, if you have too many toxins in your liver, your heart may speed up to help move things along, thus causing rapid heartbeats.

Magikal Associations

❋ **Fire** is the corresponding element.

❋ **Tongue**: The sense organ. Do you have a nasty taste on your tongue that just won't go away?

❋ **Joy** is the emotion.

❋ **Summer** is the season, and **heat** is the environmental factor.

❋ **Red** is the color.

❋ The taste is **bitter**.

❋ The direction is **south**—no argument there.

❋ Heart and small-intestine energy dominates between the hours of **11:00 a.m. and 3:00 p.m**. Do you stress during the workday and are so busy you don't take time to have lunch?

❋ Tarot card: **Strength** (heart) and **Death** (small intestines)

❋ Crystal: **Rhodochrosite**—aids spleen, kidneys, heart, pituitary gland, and circulation of blood. **Kunzite**—strengthens the circulatory system and the heart muscle. **Obsidian**—aids digestion, detoxifies, dissolves blockages and tension, including hardened arteries. **Onyx**— aids the heart.

The heart has the ability of affecting your digestion because the heart and small intestine share a close energy connection.

How can I fix my heart or small-intestine issues?

❋ SMILE! Get up in the morning, look in the mirror, and smile from your heart.

❊ When it comes to your heart, you may have to take medicine.

❊ Exercise

❊ Eat smaller portions at each meal.

❊ Drink more water.

❊ Avoid caffeine.

❊ Minimize stress.

❊ Take care of your liver to help your heart.

Spirit/Spring
Liver/Gallbladder
Ostara/Beltane/Spring Equinox

Air/Autumn
Lungs/Large Intestine
Mabon/Samhain/
Fall Equinox

Water/Winter
Kidney /Urinary
Bladder
Yule/Imbolc

Earth/
Late Summer/Solstice
Spleen/Stomach
Litha

Fire/Summer
Heart / Small Intestine
Lammas

No one knows your body like you. Take a moment now to list below some troubled traits of the heart and small intestine that you've noticed within yourself:

....

....

....

....

....

....

....

....

....

....

....

PLAN OF ACTION

What should I start doing to fix my heart/small-intestine issues? Make a list of things that you can AND WILL do. Suggestion—meditate and breathe DEEPLY. Expanding your lungs will improve heart function, but learning to breathe into your belly will help move digestion.

....

....

....

....

....

....

....

....

....

SUMMARY

Up to this point, yes, this field guide seems a bit like a diet book. But I haven't put you on a diet, nor have I given you exercises. I've shown you what to remove from your daily intake in order to feel better and relieve misery and pain from the inside out and how to apply that knowledge to your magik. Once you begin to feel more pain free, then you will be able to add exercises of your choice and diet if you so choose, but mostly you will be able to focus on your Witchy-ness so you can better serve the Goddess.

As I said in the beginning of this guide, I encourage you to continue to go to the gym . . . or massage therapy . . . or acupuncture . . . or do yoga . . . or go to your chiropractor. These things, along with this field guide, should work hand in hand to make you feel better.

As your issues subside, you should begin some sort of exercise program. Staying active is how you assist in keeping the blood flow and your energy flow moving smoothly. Keep them moving smoothly and your organs will work in harmony. If your organs work in harmony, then you should feel your best and your personal magik will be more successful.

You may hate to exercise and may refuse to do so. That's your choice. But if you could do anything at all, I would suggest stretching—such as yoga or just stretching at home. Using resistance bands can be done lying down, and working your legs, arms, and stomach can be accomplished even while watching TV. Just sayin' . . .

Chapter 3

THE INNER MAGIKAL METHOD

I've thrown a lot of stuff at you so far, but you're a Witch and can readily absorb the magikal associations. Now let's put those associations to work. Spells and inner workings are going to help with our inner and outer healings.

I've incorporated many magikal herbs for your spell work, but I'm not going to give you an entire laundry list. We're keeping it simple, focusing on just a few specific organs, and we don't want to overdo any spell work. Remember, it's the intent that matters most. A lot of high magik frills may not do anything more than something simple would do.

When you use crystals to aid in your magik, place them on the appropriate areas you want to focus on, or hold them in your dominant hand. I gave you several examples of crystals you can use. If you don't have them but have others that are good for the same thing, then use those. This is all about doing what makes you feel good and comfortable.

Some of my suggestions may not work for you. Feel free to modify and try them a different way. If after two weeks something doesn't work, try this, or try that—change it up. This is how you personalize the healing just for you. You may start feeling results right away, but mostly it takes two weeks to a month. Complete healing takes three to six months. Please give these techniques a little time and be kind to your body.

🕷 Disclaimer: Some of the herbs I'm going to list you can ingest; some you can't. Some people may be allergic to one or more of these. If you're sensitive to any of these herbs, use them only in spell work and do not ingest. If you're pregnant, think twice before ingesting herbs you've never tried before. Make sure that you consult a medical professional before ingesting, using, etc., any herb.

HEALING SPELLS FOR LIVER/GALLBLADDER

MEDITATION/VISUALIZATION

* Choose a green candle (any size or color to your liking).
* Place the Justice Tarot card where you can easily see it, and hold the crystal of your choice.
* Sit facing east (if it's a breezy day, that'll make your spell more powerful).
* Squeeze a small amount of fresh lemon juice and sandalwood oil into a dish of your liking. Add myrrh and frankincense oil for overall protection.
* Crush cloves, eucalyptus, thyme, and verbena; mix them

into your oil, and rub the mixture onto your candle.

❋ Breathe slowly in and out, clear your mind, and call forth calm. Don't let anything interrupt you while you prepare.

❋ If you want to set a magikal protective barrier in place and call in the elements, now would be the time.

❋ Light your candle, and let's begin:

Visualize your liver or gallbladder (or both) and give them a visual hug filled with love and positive energy. Notice their color. If pink and healthy, that's a good sign. If muddied, you'll need to work on them.

Now step back and imagine your blood flow. See in your mind's eye how it's moving. If it's sluggish, give it some energy.

See the blood flow moving smoother and faster, and guide it to your liver and/or gallbladder. It moves through them without getting stuck and out of your organs; the toxins that have been stuck begin to drip out.

Now see your hands. Massage the liver and/or gallbladder, starting at one side and moving down, squeezing out the toxins. As your hands move, more and more toxins come out and pool below them.

Take your time doing this and ensure you get every area of the liver and/or gallbladder.

Continue to see the blood flow moving smoothly through the organs without fail.

Once the toxins are out and in a pool, visualize flushing them out. Take them down into Mother Earth, asking Her to take these toxins and transform them into something useful and healthy for the Earth. In return, you will bring up the warm, brilliant white energy of the

Goddess and fill every part of your being.

Slowly come back to yourself, thank Deity, thank the elements, and release any protective barriers you put up for your magikal working.

After you've completed your visualization, let your candle burn all the way down. Personally, I put any leftover magiks in my burning-box collection for next Litha.

> 👁 **NOTE:** After I'm finished with this meditation I always have to pee. My body is ridding itself of toxins. That's how I know what I'm doing worked.

MAGIKAL BATH

If you're a bath person, this will work well for you.

- ❊ Draw a warm bath; light a small black candle to absorb the negativity of the illness.
- ❊ Put on some relaxing music.
- ❊ Mix grape-seed oil, lavender, camphor, and rosemary oil, and pour into your bath. Leave some for yourself.
- ❊ Sit in the bath, pour the oil in your hands, and rub them together briskly, creating heat.
- ❊ Now place your hands on your liver or gallbladder (or both) and say, three times:

Goddess heal me with your touch,
Cleanse this body I love so much,
With all I am as your domain,
Remove the sickness, heal the pain.

Once you get out of the bath and dry off,
look at the candle and say:

As this candle burns away,
Let the healing qualities stay,
By the Power of Three Times Three
This spell bound round shall be
To cause no harm, nor return on me,
And as I will, so mote it be!

Magikal Shower

Do the same as with the bath, only in the shower.

👁 NOTE: I suggest you repeat this ritual three days in a row.

Healing Charm Bag

Fashion a small bag of blue, green, and black colors,
and fill it with peppermint, chamomile,
rosemary, catnip, and milk thistle.
Hold it close. Now say the following three times:

I heal my liver, body, and soul,
I speak these words and take control,
No sickness dares to stay in me,
This little charm bag will make it flee.

Healing Spells
for Stomach and Spleen

❋ Choose a yellow candle.

❋ Place the Tarot card Chariot where you can see it, and hold the crystal of your choice.

❋ Sit facing north—no one can face the middle (sit in a way that you are comfortable).

❋ In a dish of your liking, place a base oil of extra virgin olive oil. Add myrrh and frankincense oil for overall protection.

❋ Crush angelica, chamomile, comfrey, verbena, and ginger; mix it into your oil; and rub it all over the candle. (If you don't have all of these herbs, don't stress about it. Use what you have or can easily get.)

❋ If you want to set a magikal protective barrier in place and call in the elements, now would be the time.

❋ Breathe slowly in and out, clear your mind, and call forth calm. Don't let anything interrupt you.

❋ Light your candle, and let's begin:

◇ Visualize your stomach or spleen (or both) and give them a visual hug filled with love and positive energy. Notice their color. If pink and healthy, that's a good sign. If muddied you'll need to work on them.

◇ Now step back and see the organ of your choice.

◇ How is it reacting? If bubbly or "rumbly," you'll need to calm it down. If sluggish, you'll need to give it some energy.

- ✧ Visualize cool, clean healing water running from your hands and pouring through your body.

- ✧ Wash your targeted organ, running your hands over it, gently massaging and working on cleansing and healing throughout.

- ✧ Take your time doing this. Don't rush. Start at one end and continue to the other end.

- ✧ As the stomach and/or spleen becomes pink and begins to "breathe," you breathe as well. Slow and steady.

- ✧ Imagine that leftover food, toxins, and all the stagnate things lying in your organs break down and easily flow out.

- ✧ Visually guide these toxins out of your body. Take them down into Mother Earth, asking Her to transform them into something useful and healthy for the Earth. In return, you will bring up the warm, brilliant white energy of the Goddess and fill every part of your being.

- ✧ Slowly come back to yourself, thank Deity, thank the elements, and release any protective barriers you put up for your magikal working.

After you've completed your visualization, let your candle burn all the way down. Personally, I put any leftover magiks in my burning-box collection for next Litha.

👁 **NOTE:** After I'm finished with this meditation, I always drink a cup of dandelion tea. It makes me have a bowel movement, ridding my body of toxins.

Magikal Food

Time to cook and make you well,
Natural foods go in this spell,
Stir clock wise and you will see,
Your pain will ease naturally.

✻ In a small pot on the stove, add

potatoes, peas, flax seed, a little garlic, celery, salt and pepper to taste; add some corn, just don't waste.

✻ Cook and stir until soft and done; eat a little, not a ton.

✻ If something's missing, sprinkle thyme, nothing to say, but this rhyme.

Only make a small amount. Your body uses less energy to process cooked foods, and each one of these has a magikal association.

Magikal Tea

Add to water:

❋ Slices of fresh ginger root

❋ Squeeze of fresh lemon

❋ 1 tsp. Brag's apple cider vinegar

Sip a small cup of this every day for a week, and your stomach/spleen will start to feel happier.

Magikal Desert

❋ Pumpkin pie

❋ Pineapple slices

❋ Eat either a whole or half grapefruit
every night before bed.

❋ Oranges

❋ Peaches

❋ Watermelon

Water-based fruits are best for the stomach/spleen. When ingested, they make you feel full and keep your intake under control.

HEALING SPELLS FOR
KIDNEY AND URINARY BLADDER

⁕ Choose a dark-blue or black candle.

⁕ Place the Tarot card Justice (kidney) or Star (bladder) where you can see it, and hold the crystal of your choice.

⁕ Sit facing north (sit in a way that you are comfortable) with shoulders back and down, head and eyes level; elongate the back of the neck.

⁕ In a dish of your liking, place a base oil of extra virgin olive oil. Add myrrh and frankincense oil for overall protection.

⁕ Crush elderberries, verbena, and alfalfa leaf; mix it into your oil; and rub all over the candle. (If you don't have all of these herbs, don't stress about it. Use what you have or can easily get.)

⁕ If you want to set a magikal protective barrier in place and call in the elements, now would be the time.

⁕ Breathe slowly in and out, clear your mind, and call forth calm. Don't let anything interrupt you.

⁕ Light your candle, and let's begin:

Visualize your kidney or bladder (or both) and give them a visual hug filled with love and positive energy. Notice their color. If pink and healthy, that's a good sign. If muddied, you'll need to work on them.

Now step back and see the organ of your choice.

How does it look? If black and crusty, you'll need Goddess energy to chip it away.

Visualize yourself in your warrior attire. What weapon do you carry?

Pull your weapon and approach the organ. This dark covering must come off!

Call on the brilliant, bright-white, loving light of the Goddess to shine at the tip of your weapon, and begin to hack away at the darkness.

Take your time doing this. Don't rush. Start at one end and continue to the other.

As the dark covering comes lose and floats away, your organs are revealed and begin to "breathe."   You breathe as well and release a deep sigh. Slow and steady.

Visually guide these dark pieces to leave your body. Take them down into Mother Earth, asking Her to transform them into something useful and healthy for the Earth. In return, you will bring up the warm, brilliant-white energy of the Goddess and fill every part of your being.

Slowly come back to yourself, thank Deity, thank the elements, and release any protective barriers you put up for your magikal working.

After you've completed your visualization, let your candle burn all the way down. Personally, I put any leftover magiks in my burning-box collection for next Litha.

Magikal Bath

* Fill the tub with warm water and put in all-natural Epsom salts.
* Light a small, dark-blue candle.

✳ Soak for at least ten minutes (twenty should be the maximum).

✳ Visualize toxins flowing out of you and into the bath water. Will all negativity and toxins to leave your body.

✳ When finished, stand up, pull the plug, and see it all go down the drain.

ALTERNATE: Go out into nature and put your feet and hands in a babbling stream. Visualize all the negativity and toxins leaving your body, to be carried away by the swiftly flowing water.

Witch's Glass Chant

* Get a small glass of water.

* Put in a drip of apple juice, sesame oil, and raspberry leaf (kidney) or elderberries (bladder).

* Hold the glass in your hand and, with the pointer finger of your dominant hand (or use your wand), stir the water clockwise, get a good strong swirl going, and say three times:

> I stir the items in this glass,
> Heal me now,
> Make it last,
> Berries or leaf, real and raw,
> Remove the sickness,
> Consume it all!

❋ Stare into the water and visualize your pain and discomfort being absorbed into the berries/leaves.

❋ Now finish up by saying:

By the power of 3 times 3,
This spell bound round shall be,
To cause no harm nor return on me,
And as I will, so mote it be!

❋ Now take the water away from your home and dump it at a crossroads. Yes, a crossroads, a four-way stop. Don't wait until morning. Don't wait until later on. Do it immediately! You do not want that magik water to linger in your home for too long. If you live in a city and cannot pour it at a crossroads, you can dump it down the drain and run the garbage disposal.

HEALING SPELLS FOR
LUNG AND LARGE INTESTINE

❋ Take a white candle.

❋ Place the Tarot card Lovers (lung) and/or Death (large intestine) where you can see them (use whichever you want to focus on).

❋ Sit facing west (in a way that you are comfortable) with shoulders back and down, head and eyes level; elongate the back of the neck.

❋ In a dish of your liking, mix a base oil of extra virgin olive oil with myrrh and frankincense oil for overall protection.

❋ Crush oregano, rosemary, sage, verbena, and allspice and then mix it into your oil. Rub all over the candle. (If you don't have all of these herbs, don't stress about it. Use what you have or can easily get.)

❋ If you want to set a magikal protective barrier in place and call in the elements, now would be the time.

❋ Breathe slowly in and out, clear your mind, and call forth calm. Don't let anything interrupt you.

❋ Light your candle, and let's begin:

Visualize your lungs or large intestine (or both) and give them a visual hug filled with love and positive energy. Notice their color. If pink and healthy, that's a good sign. If muddied, you'll need to work on them.

Now step back and see the organ of your choice.

How does it look? If nice and pink, you're on the right track.
But if dingy and gray, you'll have to blow it away.

Take a deep breath in, as much as you can, hold for a four count, then release. Let it all out, every bit. Now repeat ten times.

Each time you breathe in, try to expand your lungs more and more. (If working on the large intestine, breathe from your belly.)

As you do, visualize sheets of the gray loosening and lifting off.

It drifts away with every breath.

Visually guide these toxins out of your body. Take them down into Mother Earth, asking Her to take the toxins and transform them into something useful and healthy for the Earth. In return, you will bring up the warm, brilliant white energy of the Goddess and fill every part of your being.

Slowly come back to yourself, thank Deity, thank the elements, and release any protective barriers you put up for your magikal working.

You won't finish cleansing the lungs / large intestine at one sitting. You'll have to repeat this every day until they look healthy and pink.

👁 NOTE: You may want to use a long taper for this magik working. Set a time limit for how long you will work each day. Once finished for the day, extinguish the candle. Revisit this magik every day, at the same time, for the same length of time until the candle burns all the way down and goes out on its own.

Working with Air

✳ On a breezy day, stand outside.

✳ Face the wind and hold your arms open wide.

✳ Visualize yourself with holes, like Swiss cheese, and allow the air to blow through you.

✳ Inhale deeply, and as you release imagine the staleness of the organ you're working on to lift away. That strong breeze blows it up to the clouds.

✳ Calm your mind and say in your Magician's Voice:

> I call on wind, clouds, and air
> Take this sickness and leave me bare.
> Ancestors hear me from deep in your lair,
> Send me healing, send me care.

✳ Once finished, draw up the brilliant, bright-white light of the Goddess to fill the gap you just emptied, and thank Deity.

Chances are you've inherited an ailment from past ancestors. Only they know what it is to experience what you're going through. Trust that they can bring the Spirit Doctors to assist.

Lungs of the Mother

* Take a small, biodegradable seed starter pot and add in a bit of pine bark with needles (ask the tree first, though), dirt, and a little bit of water.

* Put in a few drips of healing oil of your choice, and burn eucalyptus in a burner or burn an incense stick.

* Sit it on a window sill in a strong breeze

* Focus your intent on the items and say three times:

By bark and air, water and soil
I call on the elements to infuse this oil.
Breath and flame, above and below
Let the healing begin, this sickness to go.
[Drip some more oil]
By the power of the Goddess,
I command this sickness to leave me,
As I will,
So mote it be!

Visualize your pain and/or sickness being absorbed into the little pot. Take it outside, away from your home, perhaps into the woods, and bury it deep. Walk away and DO NOT look back at it.

HEALING SPELLS FOR HEART AND SMALL INTESTINE

* Choose a red candle.

* Place the Tarot cards Strength (heart) and/or Death (small intestine) where you can see them (use whichever card you want to focus on).

* Sit facing south (in a way that you are comfortable) with shoulders back and down, head and eyes level; elongate the back of the neck.

* In a dish of your liking, mix a base oil of extra virgin olive oil with myrrh and frankincense oil for overall protection.

* Crush sage, verbena, allspice, basil, and chamomile and then mix it into your oil. Rub all over the candle. (If you don't have all of these herbs, don't stress about it. Use what you have or can easily get.)

* If you want to set a magikal protective barrier in place and call in the elements, now would be the time.

* Breathe slowly in and out, clear your mind, and call forth calm. Don't let anything interrupt you.

* Light your candle, and let's begin:

Visualize your heart or small intestine (or both) and give them a visual hug filled with love and positive energy. Notice their color. If pink and healthy, that's a good sign. If muddied you'll need to work on them.

Send a beam of brilliant white light into the Earth. Take it far, far down to the magma, the warm and pulsing heart of Mother Earth—the Goddess. Feel the heat, the energy, and the strength. Glowing hot and golden, it's full of love and peace, strength and power.

Draw that heat and energy up your beam of light and to your heart / small intestine.

Feel the warmth, strength, and peace of the Goddess filling your heart. Feel Her burning love and joy—let it fill your heart, then move out through your whole body—out to your shoulders and abdomen, into your arms and legs, all the way out to your fingers and toes, until you are filled completely with the loving light of the Goddess. This hot energy will burn away any toxins.

Now send up another beam of light into the sky and draw down the light and airy purple energy of the God. Feel the cool, sharp energy; clear and precise.

Now let the warm, loving energy of the Earth and the cool, determined energy of the heavens come together. Feel the movement of the energy within you, as they come into perfect balance and harmony.

The toxins in your heart / small intestines have been incinerated. Release the excess God/Goddess energies, keeping only what you need.

Slowly come back to yourself, thank Deity, thank the elements, and release any protective barriers you put up for your magikal working.

CHAKRA CLEANSING

Root chakra: garnet, smoky quartz, red jasper, black onyx

Sacral chakra: tiger's eye, amber, orange calcite, carnelian

Solar plexus chakra: pyrite, yellow jade, citrine, yellow jasper

Heart chakra: emerald, green calcite, amazonite, aventurine

Throat chakra: aquamarine, angelite, sodalite, blue apatite

Third-eye chakra: purple fluorite, amethyst, angelate, charoite

Crown chakra: ametrine, blue lace agate, amethyst, clear quartz

Also obtain six clear quartz crystals; any size will do.

Crown
Third eye
Throat
Heart
Solar Plexis
Sacral
Root

Lie on your back without crossing your feet, and place each of the seven stones on their corresponding chakras.

Place the six clear quartz stones in the following places: one above your head, one beside each arm, one in each hand, and one beside the feet. These clear crystals form two triangle shapes.

Relax, clear your mind, and trust that the crystals will do their work to cleanse and balance you. Relax for eight to ten minutes.

Once done, cleanse your stones. This can be done by running them under water, swishing them in distilled water, and recharging in sunlight or moonlight.

BURNING MAGIK

You can either use a long, red taper candle (which you will revisit the spell each day for a determined period of time of your choosing until the candle burns out on its own), or you can do a one-time burning, using your cauldron.

* On a piece of paper (or several pieces of paper), write exactly what it is that ails you. Be as clear as possible in a few words.
* As you write, focus your intent on ridding yourself of these things.
* Call in the quarters and set magikal barriers (you really should do this step).
* Light your candle or cauldron. Breathe. Focus.

✳ Take your time and burn each piece of paper, visualizing their destruction and release from your body. Now say:

Burn away,
From deep in me,
Release your hold,
Set me free.
By Goddess powers
And eternal light,
I will you gone,
Now begin your flight!

Chapter 4

UGH! MENOPAUSE

Don't even get me started about menopause. Ever since I hit fifty, my body went bonkers. Anything and everything started to go wrong: gaining weight, slowing down, tired, IBS, more allergies than I ever had, and the list goes on and on. And can I tell you that I've been trying to lose five to six pounds for the past six years with no luck!

So what are we going to do about it? Make a plan of action.

Exercise: Yes, I know; you don't like it or don't have time for it. But it's important! And it seems that no matter how much exercise you do, you just can't seem to tone anymore. Not unless you lift weights for an hour every single day. But you can't give up.

Have a fitness plan: It has to be one that you're comfortable with. If you can't afford the gym or know in your heart that you won't go, do some form of exercise at home. A small stair stepper will do wonders for your legs, as will floor exercises and stretching. All this you can do while watching TV. Gardening, taking a brisk walk, or riding a bike all have a place in your fitness plan.

Fitness, along with this field guide, will work hand in hand. But remember, what works for one person may not work for another. As I said in the beginning of this guide, you may need to try one thing and not another, and keep that going until you've personalized what works best for YOU.

Diet: Oh, no, the bad word! That's right, I said it. Diet. You can eat what you want, but in small portions and not in excessive amounts. Listen to your body and use my suggestions to help your body feel its best. Does your belly swell or spasm after you've eaten something? Chances are you're allergic. Omit that from future intake.

You can undertake so many plans for your menopause embattlement. Some may work. Some may not. And still, most of them will, like always, plateau. So what do you do? Learn to be happy and comfortable with YOU. Wear clothes that complement your body. Do exercises that YOU can do and fit your limitations. But you truly must adhere to a good diet and lay off all the bad stuff. Will it totally fix your menopause discomfort? No. But it will improve your overall quality of life, which is a major goal.

The positive thing I can say is that menopause is an ideal time to examine one's life, to find expression and satisfaction with work and relationships and feel committed to something larger than ourselves—to find purpose.

It's also an excellent time to cultivate self-reflective practices such as meditation and journaling.

A Few References

※ Peridot aids with metabolism.

※ Carnelian helps balance the sacral chakra, cleanse, clear, and emit healing energy to the reproductive system as it goes through this transition.

※ Citrine can help control hot flashes and balance the yin and yang.

※ Clear quartz helps with concentration and decision-making.

※ Smoky quartz can absorb and transmute the hot-flash energy, which will help cool the body.

※ Moonstone balances hormones.

※ Snowflake obsidian brings about balance to body, mind, and spirit.

※ Clary sage oil is the most effective essential oil for balancing hormones.

I'm not going to list herbs for menopause. There are a lot of them, and many you shouldn't take depending on your personal medical situation. Please do research.

As you go through menopause, you'll have to redefine your normal. The normal now is a different metabolism profile, and the level of wiggle room has decreased. What you got away with in your twenties is not happening when you are fifty plus. But it's all good. We've got this.

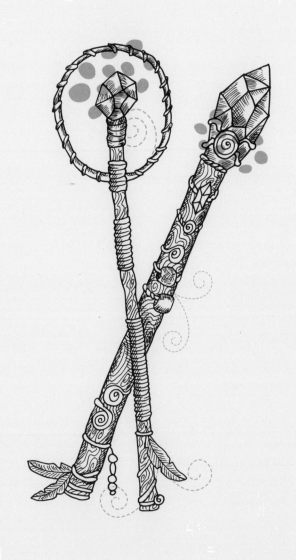

Chapter 5

SEASONS OF THE WITCH

YULE

To start off your deepest healing magik, we begin in the dark time of the year—**Yule**. At this time we pull into ourselves and battle Darkness and Shadows. In the Witch's world, Shadows refer to emotional burdens, sadness, fear, anger, and other dark (but natural) emotional states. If you harbor and/or carry these around for too long, they tend to manifest as other things—such as stress, cancer, or other illnesses.

This is a time to lay down the magikal foundation for what you hope to accomplish in the coming cycles. In other words—create a to-do list of goals. This is also our time to practice encounters with Shadow, penetrating its reality and seeing it for what it truly is.

Yule is about promise. It teaches us that life and energy go on eternally. Remember the new solar light emerges from darkness, and even in our darkest hour we can find a spark of light. Our task as Witches is to always search for that spark.

Another aspect of Yule is the interplay of death and rebirth. This is where your healing comes in. The kidney and urinary bladder dominate the dark time of the year, which goes from Yule to Imbolc. Now is the time to focus inward.

Each of us has a ritual that we like to do at this time of year. I'm proposing a basic ritual but to include healing and an encounter with your Shadow/illness/pain. As energy, Shadows cannot be destroyed, but they can be transformed.

> 👁 **NOTE:** This ritual is for the solo practitioner, but if you have a group ritual with everyone focusing on your healing, then that will make the magik that much more powerful.

Kidney / Urinary Bladder
Water / Winter

Healing Ritual for Yule for the Solo Practitioner

a. Set up your ritual space as you see fit.

b. Consecration of water and Earth

c. Consecration of air and fire

d. Cast circle with holly and jingle bells (take four sprigs of holly and place them around the perimeter of your circle). Now, as you walk around, jingle the bells and say:

> I cast this circle by the sound
> Of jingle bells all around.
> Shape for me a sacred space
> While I gather in this place.

e. Call the quarters.

f. Call in any other Gods/Goddess you desire
    (e.g., Ginisha, remover of obstacles).

g. Close the circle.

The circle is cast; this is hallowed ground.

h. Invocation: Great Mother

i. Statement of Intent

j. Walking the spiral (magik and healing)

Start music and walk the spiral. Slowly walk inward and visualize your
pain/illness leaving your body. As it lifts into the heavens, visualize that
empty spot now filled by the brilliant white light of the Goddess. Once
you reach the middle of the spiral, step over the innermost coil and
speak your wish out loud. Now slowly emerge from the spiral while
saying:

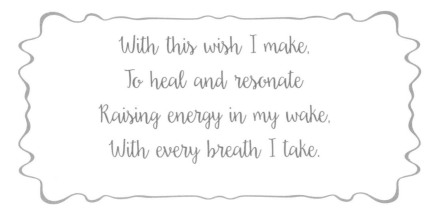

With this wish I make,
To heal and resonate
Raising energy in my wake,
With every breath I take.

When it fees appropriate, slow, and then end the chant.

- k. Cakes and wine
- l. Dismiss the quarters.
- m. Thank spirit.
- n. Ground and release
- o. Open circle: "The circle is open but unbroken; may the peace of the Goddess stay in my heart. Merry meet, merry part, and merry meet again."

 IMBOLC

Imbolc is about birth and renewal. I've included it in the dark time of the year because February is still very much winter. But under the deepest snow, a wellspring of life lay in wait to burst free!

This is a time for you to get in touch with whatever nourishes your soul. Have you abandoned reading, art, playing an instrument, or dance class because of work or life issues? The Goddess wants us to awaken our whole self. Feed yourself with the nourishment of enjoyment and the sustenance of life. Remember, you can't do that when you're too focused on being in pain, etc. We're working on healing so you can do all that you used to do and make time to get back to doing those things.

Imbolc is the time when the Earth first awakens. It's time for you to awaken too. Awakening consists of becoming present to life as it unfolds. It's not something that is happening to you; it's something that you are. Once you connect wholly, you will notice change very quickly. Though Imbolc is considered a part of spring, most of us still get a ton of snow, and darkness still lingers. It's not until near the end of February that we begin to notice that daytime lasts a bit longer—and we get hopeful.

This is also the time of Brigid: Maiden, Goddess of fire, hearth, and home, as well as Goddess of wells, springs, physicians, and healing. How fitting that Imbolc is placed on our healing pentagram with winter and water.

Brigid is also known as the Triple Goddess (maid/mother/crone), and it is at this time that some Witches create a Brigid's Cross. You may incorporate the creation of one during your ritual, if you so desire. However, I haven't included it, so please insert wherever you'd like.

> 👁 **NOTE:** This ritual is for the solo practitioner, but if you have a group ritual with everyone focusing on your healing, then that will make the magik that much more powerful.

Kidney / Urinary Bladder
Water / Winter

Healing Ritual for Imbolc for the Solo Practitioner

a. Set up your ritual space as you see fit.

b. Consecration of water and Earth

c. Consecration of air and fire

d. Cast circle with tea lights (take four tea lights and place them around the perimeter of your circle). Now, as you walk around, light each one and say:

I come in the dark, seeking light,
I come for healing and peace,
I come in perfect love and perfect trust,
I call upon your fire to purify
me with your flame.

e. Call the quarters.

f. Call in any other Gods/Goddess you desire (e.g., Ginisha, remover of obstacles).

g. Invocation: Great Mother

h. Invocation: the Inseminator

i. Close the circle.

> The circle is cast; this is hallowed ground.

j. Statement of Intent

k. Healing water (magik and healing)

Get a pan (like a long baking pan) and fill with water. Lay just the palms of your hands on top of the water. Do not submerge them. Focus on healing and ask Brigid for assistance. You hands will start to feel hot as you focus your intent. The Goddess has heard you! Once they start feeling hot say:

> By the living waters of Brigid,
> may health prevail and good reside.

When it fees appropriate, remove your hands and dry them off. Dump the water outside once ritual is complete.

l. Cakes and wine

m. Dismiss the quarters.

n. Thank spirit.

o. Ground and release

p. Open circle: "The circle is open but unbroken; may the peace of the Goddess stay in my heart. Merry meet, merry part, and merry meet again."

OSTARA / SPRING EQUINOX

Ostara / Spring Equinox is a time of birth and renewal and a time to plant the seeds of what you want to harvest later in the year. During this ritual we will focus on planting the seeds of healing and to be pain free.

This season brings faith and hope into our lives. The spiral you walked at Yule took you down inside yourself. Now is the time to follow that spiral of energy up to the light.

Signs of reawakening life can be seen everywhere as snowdrops and crocuses emerge and trees come into bud. You're ready to get outside and walk and start healing more. At this time you may feel that none of your magikal workings from Yule and Imbolc have helped with your personal health healing. I felt this too, but I didn't give up and continued to believe in the Goddess. As the year progressed, things began to happen. Remember, it takes up to six months for any magikal working results to reveal themselves.

Ostara and the Spring Equinox also focus on balance—thought, action, emotion, and spirit. Use this time to work on balancing all these things in your life. But remember, without first having chaos, you can't have balance.

Each of us has a ritual that we like to do at this time of year. I'm proposing a basic ritual but to include healing using flower seeds. You can also incorporate egg coloring, if you so desire.

👁 **NOTE:** This ritual is for the solo practitioner, but if you have a group ritual with everyone focusing on your healing, then that will make the magik that much more powerful.

Liver/Gallbladder
Wind/Spring

Healing Ritual for Ostara for the Solo Practitioner

a. Set up your ritual space as you see fit.

b. Consecration of water and Earth

c. Consecration of air and fire

d. Cast circle with colored eggs (Place four colored eggs around the perimeter of your circle. Their colors should represent what you want to bring into your life). As you place an egg at each quarter say:

> Equal dark and equal day,
> My hopes and wishes I gently lay,
> With these eggs my circle is cast,
> May love bloom, may healing last.

e. Call the quarters.

f. Call in any other Gods/Goddess you desire (e.g., Ginisha, remover of obstacles).

g. Invocation: Great Mother

h. Invocation: the Inseminator

i. Close the circle.

The circle is cast; this is hallowed ground.

j. Statement of Intent

k. Planting Our Intentions (magik and healing)

Take a small seed starter pot; add soil and a few daisy seeds. Infuse each seed with your intention of healing the organ of your choice or your entire body. Focus your will as you prepare the pot and put the seeds just under the soil. Mist them, stick a toothpick in the dirt, and tent a piece of plastic wrap to trap moisture. Now sit the pot in a windowsill to get direct sun. As you care for your seeds, you also keep the magik energy going. As the seeds grow and become healthy, you should start to feel a difference.

l. Raise energy with the snake dance.

m. Cakes and wine

n. Dismiss quarters.

o. Thank spirit.

p. Ground and release

q. Open circle: "The circle is open but unbroken; may the peace of the Goddess stay in my heart. Merry meet, merry part, and merry meet again."

 BELTANE

Beltane honors life. It represents the peak of spring and the beginning of summer. The Maiden Goddess has reached her fullness and is the manifestation of growth and renewal. This is the time for conception in all its forms. But for those who want to heal, our conception is healing magik and blessings.

We're halfway through the cycles of season, and your healing project is well underway. It's a time of action and exploiting opportunities. Are you fully committed?

Beltane is the time when nature comes alive and the Spirits of Nature are most active. It's also the time when faeries are most likely to be seen. Thus we will take advantage of this wondrous time and call forth the faerie magik of healing.

Again, Brigid is the Goddess you will call on for healing, and wishing-well magik is perfect for our healing ritual. This is the ritual when your healing magik is really going to go into high gear. After today, all sorts of things will begin to happen; you will be directed to try different forms of healing, be introduced to new techniques and supplements to try, and meet people who will guide you along the way or doctors who will finally have an answer. No matter how far-fetched it may seem, give it a try. By September you'll be feeling great! It worked for me!

This is also a time for the May Pole. New beginnings and life, sexuality and sensuality—feel free to dance around the pole to invigorate the Earth. Beltane's love is also a pure love—to love yourself. We cannot allow gender roles and the ideals/ideas of society inflicted upon us to dictate how we must look or what we must wear to be accepted, that by a certain age we should be married or have bought a house or have kids or have the perfect job. No! You must be happy with YOU. You will achieve all you wish when you're ready and when you feel the time is right. Not because you SHOULD by a certain time in your life.

Revel in this self-love and really, truly dive deep.

👁 **NOTE:** This ritual is for the solo practitioner, but if you have a group ritual with everyone focusing on your healing, then that will make the magik that much more powerful.

Liver / Gallbladder
Wind / Spring

Healing Ritual for Beltane for the Solo Practitioner

a. Set up your ritual space as you see fit.

b. Consecration of water and Earth

c. Consecration of air and fire

d. Cast circle with fairy dust. Sprinkle colored sparkles around your circle as you say:

Faeries, faeries wild and free,

I call on your powers of healing,

Join me in my circle tonight,

Let's dance together before your flight.

e. Call the quarters.

f. Call in any other Gods/Goddess you desire (e.g., Ginisha, remover of obstacles).

g. Invocation: Lady of All

h. Invocation: Lord of Life

i. Close the circle.

The circle is cast;
this is hallowed ground.

j. Statement of Intent

k. Wishing Well (magik and healing)

Set up a deep basin (flowerpot?) of some sort that may resemble a well. Fill it with distilled water. Add a few white floating candles, if you so desire, or flower petals. Next to the well have a small dish of three fairy coins (quarters). Start your music and dance around the well, raising energy and focusing on your desire to heal and be pain free. You may also call on Brigid. When you're ready, take a coin from the dish, walking around the well three times while whispering your intention. Drop it into the well and chant:

I dropped a coin into the well,
This begins my healing spell,
With my wish now set free,
Make it real, so mote it be!

You will do this for all three coins. When it feels appropriate, slow and end the chant. Now say:

By the power of 3 x 3,
this spell bound round shall be,
to cause no harm, nor return on me
and as I will, so mote it be!

l.   Cakes and wine

m.   Dismiss the quarters.

n.   Thank Deity.

o.   Ground and release

p.   Open circle: "By the four great cities of the fairy realm, my circle is open but unbroken; may the peace of the Goddess stay in my heart. Merry meet, merry part, and merry meet again."

LITHA /  SUMMER SOLSTICE

Litha / Summer Solstice is a celebration of the Goddess's power of fire. It's the time of year when everything is ripening and a time to develop the body, mind, and spirit of balance.

Litha is when you monitor your progress to see if there is anything else that you can do to help the magik you've created come into fruition. It is a time to make adjustments. Maybe those supplements aren't working. Maybe you tried what the doctor said, but feel that doing something else you read about would work better. Whatever it is, just keep going and continue to focus on your healing intentions.

Many Witches use this time to rededicate themselves to Lugh and their Path. Ask the Lord and Lady to awaken the sacred flame within your soul.

The herb Saint-John's-wort is in full bloom in June. Place a sprig of it over doorways or toss it into the solstice bonfire, to guard against faery mischief.

Witches use the energy of Litha to maintain the health of the elemental energies of fire and water within our bodies. We need this balance to quench inflamed muscles and overactive nerves.

Fire scrying at Litha is essential for a Witch to receive visions, thoughts, sounds, smells, or other sensory triggers to allow insight and direction of their Path from the Divine presence. This can be done when you burn all leftover magik bits and pieces from previous years' rituals. Use this moment to your advantage.

👁 **NOTE:** This ritual is for the solo practitioner, but if you have a group ritual with everyone focusing on your healing, then that will make the magik that much more powerful.

Heart / Small Intestine
Fire / Summer

Healing Ritual for Litha for the Solo Practitioner

a.   Set up your ritual space as you see fit.

b.   Consecration of water and Earth

c.   Consecration of air and fire

d.   Cast circle with marigolds. Place a small potted marigold at each of the quarters and say:

> *Protection, peace and love,*
> *I ask blessings from above,*
> *I cast my circle here today,*
> *Healing energy forever stay.*

e.   Call the quarters.

f.   Call in any other Gods/Goddess you desire (e.g., Ginisha, remover of obstacles).

g. Invocation: Lady of All

h. Invocation: Lord of Life

i. Close the circle.

> *The circle is cast; this is hallowed ground.*

j. Statement of Intent

k. Standing Stone (magik and healing)

Set up eight standing stones. If you have to do an indoor ritual, use potted flowers. Start the music you've selected, and weave between the standing stones, raising energy. Focus on continued healing and asking the Lord and Lady for direction on what to do next. When it feels appropriate, slow and ground and release.

l. Need Fire (magik and healing)

Take two slivers of paper. Write on one of them that which you want to give away, and, on the other, what you'd like in return. Burn the negative one and keep the positive one until next Litha. Now burn all leftover magikal items from previous rituals. Stare into the flames and focus your will.

m. Cakes and wine

n. Dismiss the quarters.

o. Thank Deity.

p. Ground and release

q. Open circle: "The wheel of the year turns and my journey continues. May the peace of the Goddess stay in my heart. Merry meet, merry part, and merry meet again."

 LAMMAS

Lammas is the first harvest festival and also the harvest of sacrifice. The first fruits are ready for picking, and the hot, humid weather imposes a slower pace so all forms of life have time to complete the cycle of growth.

This is the time to give thanks to the Lord and Lady for how your year so far has unfolded. What are you ready to reap? Remember those seeds we planted in the spring? It's time to gather some in. The rest you may need to wait until Mabon.

How does your body feel? If you've been sticking with your plan of action and following the suggestions in this field guide, you should be pain free, stomach issues should be almost or totally resolved, and you're feeling much better. As for me—this was the time of year where I felt so good I started exercising again.

Add finishing touches on new recipes or a new routine. Ask for that promotion at work or join a gym. Examine the results of your labor. It's a time to take pleasure in accomplishments.

👁 **NOTE: This ritual is for the solo practitioner, but if you have a group ritual with everyone focusing on your healing, then that will make the magik that much more powerful.**

Spleen / Stomach
Earth / Late Summer

Healing Ritual for Lammas for the Solo Practitioner

a. Set up your ritual space as you see fit.

b. Consecration of water and Earth

c. Consecration of air and fire

d. Cast circle with your athame. Walk your circle and say:

> With a grateful heart, I give thanks,
> This sacred space between Earth and sky.

e. Call the quarters.

f. Call in any other Gods/Goddess you desire (e.g., Ginisha, remover of obstacles).

g. Invocation: Lady of the Harvest

h. Invocation: Lord of the Harvest

i. Close the circle.

> The circle is cast; this is hallowed ground.

j. Statement of Intent

k. Giving Thanks (magik and healing)

Hold a small dish of grapes in your hands. Think of what you want to reap at this time. When you have it firmly in your mind, eat one of the grapes and place one on the altar as an offering. Do this as many times as you like. Also grant wishes for people you know. To add energy, you may want to dance or play drums. Once finished say:

> May my wishes and intentions
> be carried on the wind.

l. The Great Rite

m. Cakes and wine

n. Dismiss quarters.

o. Thank Deity.

p. Ground and release

q. Open circle: "My circle is open but unbroken. May I go with the peace the Goddess sends."

MABON /

FALL EQUINOX

Mabon / Fall Equinox is the harvest of thanksgiving.

This is the second harvest and falls on the Autumn Equinox—a time for balance between light and dark. After this ritual you will begin to notice that the days are shorter and nights are longer.

This is a great time to analyze your actions of the past year. Determine how successful all of your magik, rituals, and energy output have been. This assessment will help you set goals for the upcoming cycle of the seasons. It's also a good time to figure out any mistakes and problems that may have occurred; then use this information to develop a magikal solution. Decide on a resolution that you will commit to at Samhain.

We begin to reap the beauty and bounty of the Earth, and now, if you haven't already done so, it's finally time to reap the final seeds that you have sown in the beginning of the year. YAY!

Blackberries are a symbol of Brigid, and many Witches enjoy putting some in their blackberry wine for ritual. Yum! Weaving corn dolls is also a fun, magikal activity that you could incorporate into your ritual. Wine making; making jams and jellies from grapes, raspberries, and blackberries; and mixing in Kitchen Witchery are added activities. Discover how you can blend these into everyday life leading up to ritual to achieve balance and to give thanks.

After ritual, end your evening in private reflection. It's a time to complete old business as we ready for a period of rest, relaxation, and reflection.

👁 **NOTE:** This ritual is for the solo practitioner, but if you have a group ritual with everyone focusing on your healing, then that will make the magik that much more powerful.

Lung / Large Intestine
Air / Autumn

Healing Ritual for Mabon for the Solo Practitioner

a. Set up your ritual space as you see fit.
b. Consecration of water and Earth
c. Consecration of air and fire
d. Cast circle with apples. Place an apple at each quarter. Walk your circle and say:

Harvest thanks are betoken here,
The second of many for this year,
Sacred is this circle decreed,
With the riches of the Great Mother's body.

e. Call the quarters.

f. Call in any other Gods/Goddess you desire (e.g., Ginisha, remover of obstacles).

g. Invocation: Mother Goddess (Brigid)

h. Invocation: Sun King (Lugh)

i. Close the circle:

The circle is cast; this is hallowed ground.

j. Statement of Intent

k. Vine Dance (magik and healing for self and Earth)

Start the music and begin the Vine Dance, raising energy and focusing your will to continue healing. As the music ends, ground and release.

l. The Great Rite

m. Cakes and wine

n. Thank Deity.

o. Dismiss the quarters.

p. Ground and release

q. Opening the circle: "My circle is now open but unbroken. I look ahead to the darkness for rest and renewal."

 SAMHAIN

Samhain is a time to remember the ancestors, a time when the Goddess comes into her full crone aspect, and a time of transition as you begin your journey through the dark time of the year. It is your own symbolic death before renewal.

You've worked so hard on healing, you've cast out all of the bad and taken in all of the good, and you're feeling great! You may have more work to do, but the biggest and hardest part is over. Time to relax. Holidays are coming with family gatherings and all sorts of wonderful food. Enjoy, but don't go over the deep end and wind up back where you were this time last year. Remember—everything in moderation; balance and slow down during consumption.

Traditionally, this is also a time to do divination and help chart out your path in the coming year. And I totally recommend you do divination. It is also the time when the veil between the living and deceased is thin, allowing for your departed loved ones to visit.

There are many ways to honor your loved ones, and several sorts of activities you can incorporate into your ritual. This Sabat is not totally about healing; it's about reflecting on life and death. If you fear death, you cannot fully live. Every beginning has an ending, and the cycles of your life will continue in faith and unity with the love of the Goddess.

👁 NOTE: This ritual is for the solo practitioner, but if you have a group ritual with everyone focusing on your healing, then that will make the magik that much more powerful.

Lung / Large Intestine
Air/Autumn

Healing Ritual for Samhain for the Solo Practitioner

a. Set up your ritual space as you see fit.

b. Consecration of water and Earth

c. Consecration of air and fire

d. Cast circle with pumpkin candles (take four small pumpkins and carve a hole in the top big enough to place a candle. Place one at each quarter). Walk your circle and say:

> *Samhain candle of fire so bright,*
> *Consecrate this circle with light.*

e. Call the quarters.

f. Call in any other Gods/Goddess you desire (e.g., Ginisha, remover of obstacles).

g. Invocation: the Crone

h. Close the circle:

The circle is cast; this is hallowed ground.

   i.   Statement of Intent

   j.   Spirit Houses (magik and honoring the dearly departed)

During this magik you will work in silence. Take a small block of clay (either the kind that hardens on its own, or one that you need to bake in the oven to harden) and begin to tear it apart, mold it, and build a house. Make something you think your ancestors would like to stay in when they come to visit. You can make it as small or large as you like. Pour your love into your spirit house. Once it's complete, let it harden. Use it every Samhain when honoring your loved ones who have passed on.

   k.   Divination (chart your path)—use whatever form of divination you're comfortable with.

   l.   Burning (removing unwanted energy)

On a slip of paper, write down what you want to give away. On another slip of paper, write what you want in return, which will fill that void, and then put it in your spirit house. Look at it next Samhain.

   m. Dismiss quarters.

   n.   Thank Deity.

   o.   Ground and release

   p.   Open circle: "My circle is open but unbroken. The wheel of the year turns."

CONCLUSION

You finally made it through to the end, and I'm so very proud of you. I cannot stress enough that the important thing to remember is that this field guide alone will not solve all your health issues. I strongly encourage you to find a chiropractor who uses the Activator method and also incorporates the Nutrition Response Testing in their practices. Not only do I recommend this, I swear by it. This is what has helped me tremendously. It's holistic and truly works!

Adjustment and nutrition are in two parts but can be done simultaneously. Your doctor will advise which all-natural supplemental foods to take to help each organ and achieve maximum wellness. Go back to page 10 and reread about this method; do research online and ask questions of the chiropractor of your choice.

The Dragon's Way Nutrition and Exercise Program is just that: learning how to eat right using the nutrition program that has been around for centuries and incorporates Chinese exercises and theory. If there are any wellness centers in your area, please ask if anyone teaches this class. You may have to look it up online to find out where an instructor is in your location.

I took this class, and it was difficult for me to stay involved. You have to be committed. However, the Dragon's Way showed me that the organs, the energy flow, and most of the magikal associations I've mentioned in this guide all relate to the pentagram, the elements, and the Path. I learned more health philosophy than anything else, which has come in handy as I magikally grow.

Trust in the Goddess and stay open and accepting to new ways of healthy care, nutrition, and looking at how it will balance your life. When your body is healthy from the inside out, your magikal energy will flow, and then you too can be a Healthy Witch!

REFERENCES / BOOKS TO READ

Cuhulain, Kerr. *Full Contact Magick*. St. Paul, MN: Llewellyn Worldwide, 2012.

Cunningham, Scott. *Encyclopedia of Magical Herbs*. St. Paul, MN: Llewellyn Worldwide, 2006.

Hall, Judy. *The Crystal Bible*. Cincinnati: Walking Stick, 2003.

Kynes, Sandra. *A Year of Ritual*. St. Paul, MN: Llewellyn Worldwide, 2004.

WEBSITE REFERENCES

http://kitchenwiccan.com/witchs-cupboard/apothecary/

https://pagancottage.wordpress.com/our-craftings/homemade-kitchen/magickal-cooking/

http://therapeuticreiki.com/blog/crystals-for-menopause/

HERBAL REFERENCE

Disclaimer: Some of these herbs you can ingest; some you can't. Some people may be allergic to one or more of these. If you're sensitive to any of these herbs, use only in spell work (crushing and applying to candles) and do not ingest.

ALFALFA LEAF: Aids in problems that involve the digestive track and kidneys

ALLSPICE: Makes a wonderful addition to magical herbal blends for any magic focusing on increasing energy, love, healing, and luck

ANGELICA: Used for protection and purification

BASIL: Used for protection and an anti-inflammatory

CARAWAY: A mild stimulant for digestion

CHAMOMILE: An excellent herb both internally and externally for calming. Great for digestion, fevers, and burns and is an anti-inflammatory for wounds.

- Brew into a tea to aid in digestive disorders, gastritis, and difficult bowel movements.
- Blend with witch hazel and use as a skin wash to relieve dry skin, sunburns, and eczema.

CINNAMON: Used for healing, cleansing, diarrhea, dysentery, or general indigestion

CLOVE: Associated with protection, purification, mental ability, and healing

COMFREY: Very nutritious. Good for healing, protection during travel, and prosperity. Sooths the stomach and heals sprains, strains, fractures, sores, and arthritis.

ELDERBERRIES: Good for urinary issues, edema, rheumatic complaints, muscle pain

Elderberry

EUCALYPTUS: This has been a popular remedy for colds and respiratory ailments for a long time.

* Warm the leaves or oil and inhale the vapors to clear clogged sinuses, stuffy noses, and other upper-respiratory issues.

FENNEL: Aids digestion and can be chewed or brewed in a tea for weight loss, gas relief, halitosis

GINGER: Medicinally, it is used for fighting colds, calming the stomach, and suppressing nausea.

OREGANO: Can be used to soothe stomach upset, colic, and many digestive complaints. It is a powerful antibiotic and antifungal aid.

RASPBERRY LEAF: For kidney strength, infections, diarrhea, nausea, colds, and flu. Calming to the nerves as a tonic.

ROSEMARY: Magical associations include protection, improving memory, wisdom, health, and healing.

* Make an astringent out of it and use it as a skin wash to clear up your complexion, or as a soother for eczema.
* Infuse it into an oil or poultice and use it topically on achy joints and muscles, and even bruises.

ROSE HIPS: Very nutritious, high in vitamin C. Take for colds or flu; reduces fever. Mild laxative; good for acne.

SAGE: Magical associations include purification and protection, wisdom, health, and long life. Use as an antiperspirant; healing to wounds. Aids digestion and relieves muscle and joint pain.

THYME: Has been used as a cough remedy and digestive aid for ages. It can also be added to massage oils and bath oils for the treatment of rheumatism and general aches and pains. These oils can also be used for colds and lung complaints.

VERBENA: An excellent all-purpose herb to add to any spell to encourage success

Thyme

TJ Perkins has been practicing Wicca for thirteen-plus years, achieving the status of second degree and Journeywoman. While in the US Navy, TJ led aerobics and exercise classes. She professionally taught aerobics for two years, was on a high-impact aerobics team, and trained in kung fu, fencing, archery, and weight lifting. Prior Pagan picture book for ages 0–6, *Four Little Witches*, won the 2016 COVR Visionary Art Award. TJ is a gifted and well-respected author in the mystery/suspense genre for YA and fantasy for teens and children and has eight YA mysteries and a five-book fantasy series titled Shadow Legacy. A strong presence at Balticon, TJ conducts writer workshops, and the author's short stories for young readers have appeared in the *Ohio State 6th Grade Proficiency Test Preparation Book*, *Kid's Highway Magazine*, and webzine *New Works Review*. TJ's work has placed five times in the CNW/FFWA chapter book competition, and a short story of light horror for tweens, "The Midnight Watch," was published 2007 by *Demon Minds Magazine*. Adult short stories include "Redemption," The Reading Place anthology (2014), "The Sapphire Circle," "Dark Luminous Wings" (2017), "Thief in the Night," "FLASH" (2017), and more.